The Leader's Ship:

Navigating and Team Building

Charlene Free

CONTENTS

Acknowledgements……………………………………x

Foreward………………………………………….xv

Preface……………………………………………ix

Introduction……………………………………xiii

Section I: Building The Framework:……………………………………………..1

Chapter 1: What's In A Frame……………..3

Chapter 2: Brewing The Crew……………15

Chapter 3: Spare Parts…………………………23

Section II: Establishing And Managing Effective Teams………………………………………….. 34

Chapter 4: Conflict Resolution………….36

Chapter 5: The Art of Effective Communication....................44

Chapter 6: Planning To Follow And Following The Plan..53

Section III: Successfully Navigating The Leader's Ship..60

Chapter 7: Charting The Course....62

Chapter 8: A Change Of Direction 69

Chapter 9: Smooth Sailing: To Be Or Not To Be 78

References..82

ACKNOWLEDGEMENTS

I am very grateful for the plethora of leaders, who have inspired and encouraged me throughout my lifetime. Without your wisdom, support and the opportunities that you gave and still give me to practice and hone my leadership skills, I would not have the knowledge or experience base, that I now possess. You are too numerous to name, so to avoid the unpleasant circumstance of forgetting to name someone, I will simple say, THANK YOU!!! Your presence in my life, has been and continues to be, invaluable!!!

To my friends, Brother and Sister, Elders Barron and Katrina Damon. You have been my friends, encouragers, prayer warriors and business leaders. I would not have been able to complete this book in time or navigate some of the treacherous waters that I have faced in life and leadership, without your listening ears and willing hearts to lend a hand whenever I've needed you. I love you both and I treasure my connection to you!!

I am always thankful for the prayers, love and support of my pastor and his wife, Dr. Jerry and Mrs. Melvina Fryar. Thank you for always demonstrating what it means to "Lead By Example", by the way that you love and value people, beyond what you see on the outside or by what you know about their circumstances. I think very highly of both of you and I am blessed to be loved and taught by you. I love you to life!!

Thank you, Shara Hutchinson, for pushing me to GET THIS DONE and for encouraging and assisting me in the publishing process!! I appreciate you so much!!!

Gwen Williams-Wade, your presence in my life is appreciated in so many ways and for so many reasons!!! Thank you for cheering me on and for the sacrifice of your time to assist me in this process! I love you to the moon and back!!

It is easy to support someone when they are in the limelight and when things are going well for them. It takes another level of love and commitment, to stand with them, lift up their arms and their head and to value someone in their pain, when they are trying to discern how to navigate the windstorm of change, skepticism and pain. I want to thank my sisters of "Da Original Sistah Circle" Council of Presidents, Denise Johnson, Charity Martin-King, Dr. D'Andrea Mull, Deborah Pickens, Natasha Smith and Lisha West. Thank you for helping me to keep my

Leader's Ship afloat . . . When I thought I was sinking!! I love you all, from the depths of my heart!!!!

To my Great Grandmother, the Late Mother Lula Whaley, who always encouraged me and told me that I was going to do great things for God. Grandma, your influence is all over me and I am so thankful, that I had the opportunity to know and love you and to sit at your feet to learn about God and life for 35 years. I am overwhelmed with gratitude for your prayers and for all that you poured into me and for the love that you showered upon me. I love and miss you so much!!!

To my Father, who I affectionately call "Daddy", I don't have the words to fully express how I feel about you and my "Mama", the Late Gwandulyn U. Wright. The two of you have shown me love and support and guided me throughout my lifetime. You've always encouraged my writing, even from my teenage years, when I started writing poetry. You listened to my poems. Mama even asked me to write a poem for her to read on an occasion at an event. No matter what I have done or have been involved in, you have always patted me on the back, prayed for me, spoken words of life and encouragement to me and made me believe that I could do whatever I set out to do, even at times when I got tired, discouraged or just weren't sure, you said, "You can do it honey, with the Help of the Lord and we wish you the best". You've loved me unconditionally and have been present with me, for all of the milestones of my life, whether you fully understood what I was doing or not and for that, I am eternally thankful. I am so glad that God chose the two of you, to be my parents!!! I love you both to "Infinity and Beyond!!!"

Finally, TO MY LORD AND SAVIOR, JESUS CHRIST: I WOULD NOT BE WHO I AM TODAY WITHOUT YOUR LOVE, SACRIFICE FOR ME, LEADING AND GUIDING ME AND FOR PLACING YOUR WISDOM IN MY HEART AND MIND TO WRITE, TO DO, TO DREAM, TO BE, TO LIVE. I LOVE YOU WITH EVERYTHING IN ME AND I AM YOURS FOR ALL ETERNITY!!! AMEN!!

Foreword

It has been my pleasure to have known Charlene Free for numerous years, as her pastor. As partners in ministry, we share a common desire to impart insights, that develop and enrich the lives of others for effective leadership.

Every day people are doing great things in the world. What do they have in common? They all have the courage to go after their dreams, in order to make a positive impact on the lives of others. It took courage, time and sacrifice, for Charlene to move her vision to this concrete aid for more effective leadership.

Ships, navigation, crews, spare parts, organization and operational strategies, are essential elements for effectively sailing at sea. Charlene Free, has uniquely used metaphors to show parallels between these navigational components and crucial aspects of organization and strategy, for successful leadership. Her practical insights, provide invaluable knowledge to help every leader function more skillfully. I deeply appreciate the contribution Charlene has made to the field of leadership training, through this book.

Welcome, to a brief, but informative map of how to chart and stay the course, while leading others through things encountered in the sea of life. So, let's all get onboard, for an exciting time of exploration, on the voyage of leadership.

Jerry D. Fryar, D. Min.

Senior Pastor

Gospel Lighthouse Church

Columbus, Ohio

Preface

Leadership is always a challenge and an opportunity, rolled into one. It is a gift and a calling and it can lead one to be stretched in ways and directions, they never thought possible or they couldn't envision, that they would be able to bear.

Leadership is not for the faint of heart, nor for those who have tissue-textured, emotional skin. It requires knowledge and skill, a willingness to be out front and upfront, tenacity and a desire to learn and to build up others, as we are being built ourselves.

Those of us, who are willing to evolve and to challenge ourselves continuously, to do better, be better and deliver better, are the ones who possess the character and traits to effectively steer organizations and the people involved, wherever and whenever, we are leading.

As we sail together, along this journey of leadership outlined in the pages of this book, it is my hope, that each of you will come away with a renewed sense of dedication and inspiration, to lead, as you build up yourselves and others on this voyage of "The Leader's Ship" We are the captains of the organizations.

Now that you have purchased your ticket, stepped up to lead; and you have your Leadership Passport, the authority given to you by the organization that you are leading, **All Aboard . . . LET'S LEAD!!**

Copyright © 2023 Charlene Free.
All rights reserved. No part of this publication may be reproduced, distributed, or transmitted in any form or by any means, including photocopying, recording, or other electronic or mechanical methods, without the prior written permission of the publisher, except in the case of brief quotations embodied in critical reviews and certain other noncommercial uses permitted by copyright law. For permission requests, visit the website below.

ISBN: 979-8-37644508-2 (Paperback)

www.flo2life.com

Section I:

Building The Framework

What's In A Frame?

Every leader must know and understand the mission and end for which they are leading.
Failure to understand this, leads to disappointed and misguided direction. These things translate into wasted time and efforts, as well as stagnation and underdevelopment of the organization involved. Therefore, a wise leader understands that there are essential parts - people, departments and resources, that must be assessed and evaluated prior to launching a vision or taking action on a project. For the purposes of this writing, the word, "organization", will be used for all leadership references, throughout the book. However, the information within this book, is useful for and pertinent to leaders of committees, departments, boards, charitable organizations and community service groups, businesses, churches, and corporations.

Ships, have many parts. Some parts are visible, while others remain invisible to the observer. Some of the visible parts consists of the rudder, anchor, bow, keel, accommodation, propeller, mast, bridge, hatch covers, bow and the roosters. While other parts, such as the bulkheads, frames, cargo holds, hopper tank, double bottom, girders, cofferdams and side shell, remain invisible. Just as the ship will not operate optimally without all of its parts, the organization will not maintain or establish its' optimal level of operation, without those who are leading out front and those who are performing all of the necessary tasks that are paramount, to the organization's ability to thrive and succeed. Therefore, the effective leader must realize the importance of demonstrating appreciation and respect, for all teammates, regardless of the types of jobs they perform. Careful attention must also be given to the maintenance of teammates through vision casting with leaders and cultivating an atmosphere in which all teammates have the opportunity to learn, grow and be heard. Incorporating this can be a challenge, especially for large organizations and corporations. Those in leadership who dare take on the challenge of operating this way, will, however, build a legacy of leadership that lends itself to expansion of teams inwardly and outwardly as individuals and as viable parts. An atmosphere will be created that will cause teammates to follow the leader because they want to and not because they have to. Yes, there will be those who will not want to follow the designated leader, no matter how much is done or no matter how much support they are given.

These challenges will become less and less and will be few and far between, when the ship is steered from a standpoint of mutual respect and support. However, these instances will become less and less, when the leader demonstrates respect and support for each person's role, even in the face of disagreement and inevitable change.

Every ship has three essential parts: the hull, the navigation bridge, and the engine room. The Hull is the main body of the ship. It gives the ship its shape and keeps water out. The hull of every organization, is what gives it relevance, purpose and validity of existence. Every organization, must have a purpose statement, criteria or statements and guidelines that govern how the business will operate, core values and goals as to the purpose of its existence and from which to build upon and operate. These things are a collection of "whys" - why the organization exists, and why and how it intents to function. It is the very foundation for the organization's formation and coming into being and it will greatly provide direction and for charting the intended course. The organization must be established and maintained upon a strong foundation. Therefore, it is necessary to formulate the purpose, core values and goals in writing and to ensure that each teammate understands these principles and the vitality and validity of how their perspective roles, assure and aid in the process of the organization's overall success.

The Navigation Bridge, is the command center of the ship. It controls speed, and direction, tracks weather and sea conditions and the navigation and fixation of the position of the ship, while facilitating internal and external communication. The leader must have, establish, maintain, and be able to execute the direction and vision that has been cast by the owners, board, themselves - if this is an entrepreneurial adventure, or the founders. No organization, can flourish without a leader who knows and understands how to direct its operations with the needed changes additions, etc., that arise with time, just as a ship will lose its direction without a well- equipped and operational, Navigation Bridge and its crew members. If the organization, has a leader who does not know the necessary pathway of navigating towards success, it will lose momentum, good team members/staff, committee members, etc., and will eventually, lose profit, positive visibility, their competitive edge and will cease to be relevant in the community or the marketplace. The leader does not monitor or affect the direction of the ship, solely. Rather, the leader relies upon their knowledge and skills, as well as the collective knowledge and skills of their executive leadership teammates and their respective teams, to avoid these difficulties.

    The Engine Room, is the heart and soul of the ship. It is not visible to the observer. It propels the ship and helps to keep it moving. Those who work in the engine room of a ship, maintain, operate and repair the engine.

Adequate and accurate performance of the engine, ensures that the ship will remain operational. Deficits in this area, will lead to peril of the survival of everyone aboard. The captain is responsible for the overall management and oversight of the entire ship. In an organization, the "engine room", represents those whose work may go unsung and unnoticed, with very little thought given to their importance of being.

However, if they are not in place and performing their assignments as intended or outlined, it can be very difficult or impossible, to navigate the organization to its intended destination.

It is very important that all teammates, regardless of whether or not, they are considered to be in leadership, understand and execute, what I call, "The ENERGY", of the organization. This acronym stands for:

- **E:** Excellence in action
- **N:** Necessary insight
- **E:** Enough to keep going
- **R:** Relevance and a Resilient Stride
- **G:** Gravitational Grounding
- **Y:** Yield To Increase

This ensures that everyone works toward the expectation and demonstration of:

    A. Operating with **EXCELLENCE** in their roles
    B. Providing **NECESSARY** insight and feedback for the good of all.

  C. Ensuring that they are doing **ENOUGH** to keep the operations of the organization running as smoothly as possible.
  D. Exhibiting understanding of the **RELEVANCE** of their function in correlation to other departments, parts, etc. and exercising a **RESILIENT STRIDE** in the face of realignments and adjustments necessary from time to time.
  E. Continual **GRAVITATION** towards the intended goal or destination, while exercising emotional **GROUNDEDNESS**.
  F. Being willing to be a team player by understanding the need to sometimes **YIELD** to a different mindset or way of doing things, in order to achieve **INCREASE** for all!

  Every leader, Captain of the Leader's Ship, must possess this "ENERGY", personally and have the ability to infuse this into the organization. True leadership is a privilege and a calling to a deeper level of service. The importance of leadership is not just the perks, financial gain or the accolades; although all good and effective leaders tend to experience these things at some point on their leadership journey of life. So the question becomes, did you choose leadership, or did it choose you? There is a difference. Those who choose leadership, are dedicated to lifelong learning and improvement. They see the importance of their leadership beyond themselves. It is a sacrificial journey that brings growth and a wealth of opportunities to them and to those that they are leading or serving. It is different than being chosen by leadership. Those who are chosen by leadership, have received it by default, inherited it or were talked into leading, without really having the necessary tools, mindset and heart to lead. This difference becomes more profound, as the winds of time and change begin to blow, and the leader has experiential challenges that cause them to stretch, become uncomfortable at times and to think outside of the traditional leadership box. A person who chooses leadership, even if it didn't begin that way, but evolved with time, experience and training - will be able to withstand the myriad of tests and growth experiences that accompany the role of leadership. Those who allowed leadership to choose them, may falter under the weight that leadership may bring, unless they are willing to undergo a leadership evolution and transformation of their mindset, heart of leadership and skillset acquisition.

Great leaders recognize that they must have the essentials for an effective navigation of their Leader's Ship. Therefore, the framework must be adequate and appropriate or have the ability to attain this status, in order to breed the rewards of success for all involved.

Just as the wise captain ensures that these three parts are in tact before setting sail, a leader must make a self-assessment and an assessment of the place of leadership, into which they are about to ascend, prior to taking or assuming the helm or shortly, thereafter.

A frame with missing or damaged parts, is a sure recipe for a sinking vessel. Such is the case for any organization, if the foundation is weak or substandard. Therefore, it is paramount to assess the frame by understanding the foundational rules, expectations, budgets, etc. Evaluate your frame. Know your capacity for leadership. Are you able to lead projects, organizations, operations, events, committees, groups, etc., on the level for which you are asked? Are you able to be effective without losing sight of the big picture and yourself, in the process? Do you have an adequate number of teammates to carry out these tasks? Do they have adequate knowledge in their perspective roles, to proceed in the necessary operational tasks? This information and more, is pivotal to your success and the organization's success, whether it is a large or small endeavor. Your final step before you begin, should be to go on a quest to thoroughly understand the ship that you are leading, every component, and the goals towards which, you are setting the course.

After all of these assessments have been made and examined and you
are confident in your steering abilities for this voyage, get ready and get set, to begin your journey of leadership and team building!

LEADERSHIP PROBE:

1. How will you navigate a new team, or organization, that needs help crafting their mission statement or purpose?

2. If the frame is broken, and the organization needs rebranding, has rapid turnover, lacks the necessary funds to keep moving forward, etc.; what strategies can you use to repair the frame?

3. What can you do to bring stability to a group you are leading, whose priorities are constantly changing or who is in flux?

STRATEGIES AND RECOMMENDATIONS:

1. **Crafting Statements of Mission and Purpose:**
   A. Knowing this information will help you and your leadership team craft a vision or a mission statement that will demonstrate or convey what the organization is about and what it seeks to do.

2. **Broken Frame Repairs and Assessments: Make a checklist of priorities in 1-3 month increments. Be realistic in strategy and execution.**

A. Survey all team members, groups members, etc., about what the group or business does well or what it needs to improve upon. Be sure to address their concerns individually and as a group, as far as you are able to and within reason, whether you agree with their statements or not. Be determined to give everyone a voice, without taking anything that is said, written or done, personally.

   B. Be honest with stakeholders, owners, etc., if the entire frame needs an overhaul, be prepared to present your proposal in writing, but as a schematic, not in its final form. This will allow you to receive vital feedback, which is necessary for a win-win.

A. Have an open and honest discussion with all involved regarding the importance of establishing and sticking with priorities, in order to promote respect in the community and marketplace, attract new members or team members, increase sales, etc. Consider stating that riorities can be re-evaluated every 6-12 months, but stress that consistency in execution, is the key to overall success.

Brewing The Crew: Establishing An Effective Team

Now it's time to take a look at the people who are involved in this voyage of your leadership. Let's begin by gaining an understanding of the jobs and responsibilities of crew members on a actual ship. You will find that some of these positions correlate to one or more positions within an organization.

The Captain: Is a person, who is licensed to sail or direct a marine vessel. This person provides overall command and control of every aspect of the ship and its voyages. As the **(Leader, President, Chief Executive Officer (CEO), Pastor, Board Chair, etc.)** you are the captain of the leader's ship.

The First Mate or **Chief Mate:** Is the 2nd in command of the ship. They coordinate and supervise the day-to-day activities of all members. They are in charge of the cargo and the passengers. **(Vice President, Chief Operating Officer - COO)**

The Second Mate: Maintains navigation charts, instruments and publications. They are in charge of navigation. **(Executive Leadership Team Members, Data Researchers, Strategic Planning Management Team, Risk Management Team)**

The Third Mate: Officer of the watch. Assists in oversight of the ship's maintenance. A junior officer in the deck department that trains cadets. **(Department Manager, Committee chairman, Supervisor)**

Deck Officer: Maintains watch on the bridge. Responsible for passage planning, safe navigation of the ship, cargo loading and discharge, ship stability, communication of the hull and deck equipment. **(Strategic Planning and Risk Management Team, Board Members, IT Team, Committees/Sub Committees, Various Departments)**

Boatswain: Deck boss. Most senior member of the deck crew. Supervises, schedules and assigns work and crew members. Regularly inspects the ship. **(Area Director/Managers)**

Chief Engineer: Supervises all engineers, oversees all operations, and maintenance of the engineering department. **(Team Leads, Department Heads)**

Watch Leader: Supervises, maintains discipline for a watch team of sailors. Ensures that the right leaders, are doing the right jobs, at the right times. **(HR Managers, Quality Control, Risks Managers)**

Able Seaman: Must have more than 2 years of experience at sea. Assists with customer service, ship operations, etc., as needed. **(Admins, Customer Service Personnel)**

Purser: Manages finances, orders supplies, etc., as needed. **(Accounting/Finance Team, Procurement Team)**

Chief Steward: Directs team members who work as cooks, cleaning crew, places orders, etc. **(Maintenance Team, Workers)**

This is not an exhaustive list of positions, roles or responsibilities. Rather, it serves as a comparison between members of a ship's crew and teammates of an organization. As the organization grows or is being formulated, hiring personnel, obtaining resources, etc., the necessity of having a Board of Directors, Executive Leadership Team, etc., will come into play. A skilled crew, who operates with each person, effectively executing their assigned tasks, will assist in securing the firm foundation and grounding, which is necessary for successful navigation. The collective experiences and wisdom that come from the leaders who comprise these groups, is invaluable, provided that they have the heart and mind to lend themselves to doing and being what is required.

You may inherit a board or executive team. It will be imperative to work cooperatively with them while you are learning and executing the organization's vision. As you continue your leadership, it will also become necessary to add to your departments and committees. A wise and confident leader understands the advantage and necessity of choosing leaders, who are skilled in areas, in which he or she, is not. They are not intimidated by those who are more successful, skilled or influential than they are. They know and lead with the end game in mind.. . . . SUCCESS of the organization and for all of the team members involved!! As a lifelong learner, the leader continues to strive for upward mobility of their own leadership, which requires building upon experiences, receiving and adhering to the advice and mentorship of others, as well as learning from those with whom they surround themselves.

One of the ways to maintain a team dynamic, is to operate as a transformational leader. Transformational leaders are focused on growing and investing in people and not just on striving for financial gain and influential notoriety, even though these are important components of the success and continuance of any organization.

A Transformational Leader specializes in continued growth and maturity within themselves and within those that they lead. They constantly adjust their leadership style, to ensure that they are able to lead
each team member towards organizational and personal excellence.

They are keenly aware, that their particular leadership approach, cannot be cookie cutter. Rather, it must lend itself to the concept of being understood and approachable by all and must empower each teammate working with them, to execute the overall mission of the
organization, with clarity and excellence. Transformational Leaders seek to be authentic in communication, interactions and engagement of those that they are leading. When all of these parts are blended together, this allows the leader to bring people and resources together in a way that perpetuates a meaningful voyage for all involved.

Leadership Probe:

1. What do I do, if I inherit a board or executive leadership team who is difficult to work with or who will not adequately perform their duties to the organization?

Answer: Section III, Chapter 2, addresses this question.

2. How can I ensure that I have managers, supervisors, etc., on board with the right skillset for the organization? How can I make certain, that they are the right fit?

If you are leading a corporation, establishing a community group or leading an established organization, make sure that you have a Human Resources Director and team who understands and is committed to the vision, core values and mission of the organization. Do all that you can to ensure that they understand the importance of bringing onboard, those who are highly qualified for their prospective positions, but who also understand the culture of the organization and what you are trying to execute, relative to the business or projects that you are involved in. Make clear, the expected team dynamics you wish to have displayed on a daily basis. Remember, the goal is to create a culture people WANT to stay connected to. Offer trainings and encourage team members to continuously seek professional development. Annually allocate funds to pay for and provide reimbursement for pre-approved coursework that match the needs and values of the organization. If you are a start- up and cannot afford to provide these supports, look for community leaders who are trained in certain areas, that may be willing to offer free or affordable professional development.

Evening workshops and Lunch and Learn events are great ways to invest in and inspire your team. Finally, keep in mind that you don't have to know or do everything. Just make
sure that you have people around you, who are excellent at what they do.

Spare Parts

Every captain knows that sailing is a wonderful and rewarding experience. There are destinations to be discovered and rediscovered. However, the wise captain knows that prior to launching the voyage, there must be an acquisition of spare parts, in the event of an emergency or if the vessel will remain out to sea for an extended period of time. Ensuring the presence of the ship's manual is essential, in the event that a part must be procured during the voyage. Spare parts are necessary, in order to maintain the integrity of the vessel and to keep everything in good working order. However, they are not used, unless they are needed to replace another part.

In the shipping industry, suppliers often speak different languages. Therefore, parts by the same name, could have a different part, drawing or item number, which can vary from manual to manual. Manuals are updated often, but the material number, is the most definitive way to identify the part. The part numbers often change. The details of the material number, are not usually shared in manuals, in order to protect trade secrets. Descriptions and details are often required, because these numbers, parts, drawing or item numbers, are not sufficient to describe the part, in totality.

Within every organization, there are people who play vital roles in launching and maintaining the goals and mission of the owners and the organization itself. Although the roles of the teammates are different, all are needed in some capacity. Effective leaders, know the capabilities of their team, just as the wise captain knows the capabilities of their crew and provides opportunities for growth, learning and promotion within their ranks. Let's examine two scenarios to illustrate the importance of being a leader who knows how to effectively utilize this knowledge.

Susan, is a very dedicated team member. She's always on time, energized and completes her assignments with excellence. However, she is not a member of the managerial staff. Her friend Mike, has started to notice that Susan hasn't been herself lately. She has become quiet and reserved and doesn't spend as much time around the team as she used to. One day, Mike decides to pull Susan aside to inquire about the changes he has noticed.

Mike: "Hey Susan", can I talk with you about something for a minute"?

Susan: "Sure". Mike finds a private area during their break.

Mike: "Susan, I've noticed that you've been really quiet lately and I don't see you very much anymore. Is everything, ok?"

Susan: "Yeah, I've just been thinking about a lot of things. I've been here 10 years and I'm still doing the same job. I've never been offered a promotion, but I have a lot of great ideas that I know could improve some things. No one ever asks me what I think about anything. I'm not a manager and I am not trying to step on anybody's toes. I just know that I can do more and be more, if given the chance. Oh, what does it matter! I'm just a spare part, so I sit back and say nothing, but it's really starting to bother me more and more".

Mike: "Wow", I had no idea, but I wanted to ask what was going on, from a friend, to a friend.
   Say, why don't you set a meeting with your manager. Just tell him that you want to talk to him about some ideas you have. You never know what will open up for you."

Susan: "Mike, you're right, I need to do that. I will never know until I try. Thanks!

Susan went back to her office and sent her supervisor, a message, to request what she called, a "brainstorming session." Jim replied and gave her a date and time to meet, three days later.

On the day of the meeting, Susan was so excited! She knew that her ideas may not have actually taken shape, but maybe some of them would be put into action and if nothing else, Jim would be aware of her ideas, which may cause him to see other capabilities she had beyond her current role and job description. The meeting was set for 10 a.m. Susan walked to Jim's office, notes and pen in hand, ready for a productive exchange.   Mrs. Lampkin, Jim's administrative assistant, greeted her and walked her into Jim's office. Jim: "Hi Susan, come on in and take a seat", Jim said. Susan tried to contain her enthusiasm, but her face beamed with excitement!

Susan: "Hi Jim, thanks for meeting with me on such short notice."

Jim: "No problem Susan. You said that you wanted to have a brainstorming session. So, what can I do for you?" Susan began to outline her ideas to Jim and provided explanations as to how each idea could benefit their department and ultimately, the company. After she finished speaking, Jim was silent for a few seconds.

Then he said, "Susan, you have put a lot of time into this and I know that your intent is to benefit the department. The problem is that although your ideas are good, we don't usually take these kinds of recommendations from anyone who is not in management.

They come to us with suggestions and recommendations, along with the proposed budgets and the manpower to help us put their proposals into action. The fact that they are managers and they have a team that can research the items further, if we request them to do so, is a win-win for all of us. We depend on their years of experience and expertise and many of them have assisted us with making some effective improvements, so their results are tried and true. I want you to know that you are valuable to this department. Please   hold on to those suggestions. In the event that you are promoted into management, we can review them again. Is there anything else you would like to discuss?

Susan: "No. But thank you for your time. Again, I appreciate the meeting", Susan said, trying
         not to let her face display the deflation of exuberance she felt inside.

Jim: "Sure thing, anytime."

Susan: "I knew it, I really am just a spare part! From now on, I'm not going to share anymore ideas, unless they ask me to. There is no use in sharing them, so I will keep them to myself."
These were Susan's words to herself as she closed the office door, walked back to the elevator, got off on the 3rd floor and walked back to her cubicle.

At another business across town, Michelle waited for an 11 o'clock appointment. One of the teammates in her department, asked if she could have a 30 minute block of time, to share some suggestions. At exactly 11, Mrs. Jones, her administrative assistant, showed Marcy into her office.
Michelle: "Hi Marcy. Please come in."

Marcy: "Thank you, Michelle. I know you have other meetings today, so I will get right to the point."
Marcy shared her ideas and suggestions with Michelle on possible expansion of the team and other quality improvement measures. Michelle listened intently and when Marcy was finished, Michelle thanked her for taking the time to share her thoughts.

Michelle: "Marcy, I really appreciate what you've shared. We may be able to incorporate two of your suggestions with our present infrastructure.

I am not sure that we will be able to implement all of the other topics you spoke on, but I am quite impressed that you thought of them and happy that you shared
them with me. Have you ever considered taking any of our in-house certifications? They are designed to prepare our team members for management positions, which may need to be filled in the future."

Michelle: "No", I really hadn't thought about it before now." Michelle handed her a pamphlet with descriptions of the certifications, information on which managerial positions they corresponded to and how to sign up for them. Marcy was very surprised and excited to receive this information. She thanked Michelle for her time and for sharing the information.

Michelle smiled and said, "I look forward to hearing about your progress and the benefits you receive from the certifications." Marcy left Michelle's office feeling invigorated, heard, valued and empowered.

These scenarios had some similarities. Both centered around good team members, who were dedicated to their organizations, and who had ideas and suggestions to share for the benefit of their departments within those organizations. In the first scenario, appreciation of the team member was spoken. Appreciation was spoken in the second scenario as well, but it was also demonstrated.

Leaders who take the time not only to hear those that they lead, but also to assist them in becoming more successful in their current roles and possibly to be promoted into a higher level of responsibility, are leaders who know how to decrease, if not nullify, the "Spare Parts Syndrome". It is a given that there must be those who do the foundational work within an organization in order to keep it thriving and on the cutting edge.

No organization will be successful without its team members. It is also true that there are those who only try to climb the ladder to promote their own self- interests, with no regard or respect for the direction or purpose of the organization or what is best for the whole. Every leader must deal with this type of peril at some time or another. The leader who is intent on successful navigation of their organization is keenly aware that conflict management is more than simply managing conflicts among team members and departments. There are times when this it is also necessary to assist team members who are managing their own internal conflicts relative to their worth within the organization and with helping seeds of leadership grow and blossom when they are presented. This type of leadership, keeps fresh vision, ingenuity, and the waters of success, free flowing and purpose driven.

LEADERSHIP PROBE:
1. How can you cultivate an environment that seeks to prevent the "Spare Parts Syndrome"
    A. Create an atmosphere, which allows people to be heard without criticism. SPECIAL NOTE: THIS DOES NOT MEAN THAT YOU TOLERATE DISRESPECT IN ANY FORM! Make sure that adequate guidelines are set and understood for being heard. Do this early on.

    B. Have an open door policy, but not a revolving door policy. Make sure that those you are leading, have a good understanding of when you will be available to meet with them and it is best to operate by appointment. Set reasonable office hours and establish ways to gain an audience, via an online platform, in person or by phone. Do not allow ongoing conversations, for which a decision has already been made, is permanent, or cannot be reversed. Provide one to two verbal or written clarifications if they do not understand the matter. But be cautious of investing too much time re-explaining what you've already stated, verbally, in writing or in meetings.

2. Set up an active pipeline to cultivate leadership efficacy, development, and promotion. Work with or establish an effective leadership development team, who seeks to identify potential new leadership and to train and encourage current leadership. Create and maintain a culture that seeks to recognize and promote new and existing leaders into potential new roles. Remember, a ship that doesn't provide room for new parts and maintenance of existing parts, will sink. Such is the case with organizations and groups alike.

Section II:

Establishing And Managing Effective Teams

Conflict Resolution And Management

Tyrone: "Sandra, your fundraising efforts, don't align with what my team has proposed for our community engagement projects this year. I really wish that you had talked to me before presenting this. The amount that you are projecting will only allow us to have 3 projects. We have already made plans for 5."

Sandra: "Well, this is all of the money that we expect to raise, given the state of the economy. Current trends show that businesses and corporations have decreased their charitable giving and my team and I thought that it was best to propose an amount that was within reason and safe to project, rather than to overestimate and place the organization at risk of not being able to deliver or to go over budget."

Tyrone: "Well, our communities can't play it safe with their needs, which is supposed to be our overall goal, meeting THEIR needs, remember?"

John, the Board Chair:" Hold on, both of you. Our goal is to do both. Meet the needs of the community and to stay within budget, but we will not be able to move forward, without resolving this. Sandra, you have done a wonderful job of chairing our fundraising committee over the last few years. Tyrone, the projects that your team organizes for community engagement, have been very impactful! I recognize the importance of the work that both of you and your teams, do. Rather than continuing the debate over this, I am asking the two of you to take some time, regroup, get together and formulate a strategy that will bring resolution to this in a manner that allows all of us to continue working together cohesively. If either of you wants to meet with me individually or collectively, prior to our next board meeting, I will make myself available for that. Just let me know and we can set a time to do that. For now, we will move on with our next order of business and revisit this discussion at the next meeting."

Fast forward, 30 days later:

Tyrone and Sandra took the next several weeks individually, to settle down emotionally from this topic. They also decided to meet for a brainstorming session, in order to begin preparations for the next board meeting.

John initiated the meeting. He and Sandra met for an hour one evening and this is how their interaction unfolded:

Tyrone: "Hi Sandra, thank you for agreeing to meet this evening. I know that we need to talk and try to resolve our differences.

Sandra: "Thanks for initiating the meeting, Tyrone. Yes, we definitely need to get things ironed out. I want you to know that I didn't mean to step on your toes and draw a line in the sand with my presentation. My team and I were trying to propose what we thought was doable, but I didn't think about how this may have come across to you as not being considerate of the work that you and your team do."

Tyrone: "Thanks for saying that, Sandra. I don't want you to have the impression that I don't appreciate what you and your team do, to keep us fiscally sound. I was just thinking about the needs of the community and when I heard the proposed amount, I was focused on what may go undone, rather than all of the other parameters. So, how can we move on from this and what can we do to make sure that we do our best to avoid this misunderstanding again?"

Sandra: "We could put in place, having a joint team meeting, 3 months before the end of our calendar year, so that my team can hear your team's thoughts and ideas, give insight on remaining funds from the year and talk about potential funding sources, relative to the proposed community engagement plans for the following year."

Tyrone: "We could also do some research on potential funding sources that have been untapped and we could also look into collaborating on some community engagement projects that are at the heart of our core values, but where we may be able to partner with another organization who is involved in similar projects and if we are able to make that connection, it would reduce our cost of funding some projects."

Sandra: "Great idea!! Well, because we are in the midst of this right now and we need to have something viable to present next month at the board meeting, is it possible that we can schedule a joint meeting with our teams in the next week or two to discuss possibilities of collaborative efforts in bringing all of this to fruition?"

Tyrone: "Absolutely! Please look at your teams ' calendar and send me some dates over the next few days. We will make it happen."

Sandra and Tyrone took the rest of the hour, to talk about several items that they could present to their teammates during the upcoming, joint meeting. The meeting was scheduled, the teams collaborated, and Sandra and Tyrone were able to strategize for the next board meeting on a joint presentation. They gave information to board members, which included a revision of budget projections and projects, whose costs could be reduced by forming community partnerships and combining some of the organization's current projects. The board agreed to their updated proposals, and it was a peaceful resolution for all involved. Additionally, Tyrone and Sandra decided to maintain the joint meeting of their teams, twice a year, rather than just the initial one proposed for 3 months from the end of the calendar year. This allowed both

teams to gain a greater understanding and respect for what the other team does and to assess progress and status of projects and fundraising efforts/financial standing, mid and end of year.

Every organization, and every team, will face conflict at some time. There will be differing opinions and thoughts, which often emerge from previous experiences with other entities; and there will be various trends of thought that arise in the moment. HOW these differences are mitigated, will make all the difference between navigating an obstacle and creating or perpetuating a toxic, work, or operational environment.

No one wants to serve or work in an environment where there is chaos, gossip, continuous strife, a lack of professional respect, or moral and ethical anarchy. This can result in unresolved issues. Sometimes, people leave an organization that they greatly love, because they cannot, or are no longer willing to, tolerate the toxicity of the environment or the people involved. There are also times when one or more leaders is so passionate about the work that they are doing, that their tone and the come across is reflected negatively. Not because they are careless, but because they care so much about the work that is being done/who is being helped. It is easy to become angry regarding what we are passionate about, when we feel that needs are being ignored, However, the leader must exercise optimal emotional intelligence to make these kinds of explosions the exception and not the norm.

Peace is not the absence of conflict. It is the successful navigation through and in spite of the conflict that brings peace and a workable solution. All organizations with an HR department, have established ways and mechanisms in place to handle conflict resolution. However, if you are leading a start-up or organization, which has no HR team, you may need to make yourself available to assist teammates with solving conflicts, just as John did in this scenario.

Avoid taking sides and you don't want or need to get involved, unless it is necessary. Proactively, it is good to make yourself available and to make it known that you value both parties and that you are willing to assist. Unless there has been a violation of something or a serious interaction in the meeting that must be addressed, allow them to initiate a meeting with you, instead of you setting a meeting with them. Many times, people are able to work things out on their own, but everyone appreciates knowing that they can approach the leader without scrutiny and with confidence and confidentiality.

Encourage teammates to take cooling off periods, rather than to continue discussing or debating the issue. This may avoid an explosion or potential fire at sea, of your leader's ship. Rather than maintain their focus on each other's differences, remind each of them of the potential and positive things that each person brings to the table. Encourage them to think about the similarities they have, and how they can and do support each other's work. Demonstrating this type of leadership will help your teammates work more cohesively today, rather than attempting to throw each other overboard or demanding each other to "walk the plank", metaphorically speaking, because they are unable or unwilling, to work together for the good of the whole.

The Art of Effective Communication

Communication is essential to all living creatures. Without it, no member of the animal family or human race, would be able to exist or maintain itself in the intricate world and its dynamics, in which they live. Just as this is true and evident in our world of life, so it is in the world of leadership and business.

Communication is defined as the imparting or exchanging of information or news. It is further defined, as the means of sending and receiving information, and as a process by which, information is exchanged between individuals or entities, through a common system of symbols, signs, or behavior. It may be spoken or written language or a series of codes or body language. Regardless of the mode of communication the sender chooses, it must involve a recipient in order to be rendered as a communicated message. In other words, communication, is a two-way street. Without this understanding, it can become cumbersome, confusing, ineffective and a waste of time.

There are times when a captain needs to communicate with the crew or other vessels. It is essential that this communication is clear and concise when transmitted to the receivers. This is especially important to avoid danger and disaster at sea.

Crew members may be from different parts of the world, therefore, it became necessary that a common system of communication be developed and utilized among all mariners.

In 1983, a group of linguists and shipping experts, created a system of communication called, "Seaspeak". English was chosen to be the primary language because it was the most common language spoken at that time and because it was also the language of civil aviation. In 1988, the International Maritime Organization, made Sea speak, the official language of the seas. Seaspeak defines the rules of how to talk on the radio and the number of words that can be used is limited, to ensure that messages are short and clear. For communication to be effective within an organization, it must be clear, concise and relayed in a way that is easily understood. Just as the use of Seaspeak, aids in the avoidance of disaster at sea, appropriate and adequate communication can avoid wreckage of the leader's ship.

We will examine several types of communication in this section. Let's begin with Interpretative Communication. This type of communication is presented in such a way, that the originator of the communication sends it in any mode, with the expectation that the recipient will be able to extract intent and meaning in the way that key words, ideas, emotions, thoughts, goals or expectations are conveyed, will be understood and possibly, acted upon by the recipient, without further input from the sender. It is one-way communication and the receiver is taxed with figuring out or deciphering meaning, input of emotions, tone, next steps, etc., on their own. There is no two-way exchange in this mode of messaging. Text messages, emails, notes, and voicemail messages, are examples of interpretive communication.

Interpersonal communication allows the sender to convey thoughts, ideas, goals, expectations, feelings, etc., in verbal and non-verbal ways. It incorporates all language aspects, verbal language, facial expressions, body language, tone, and gestures. It involves active listening and the giving and receiving of feedback on the original message conveyed. It lends itself, to a series of exchanges between the sender and the receiver, that can provide clarity to all involved.

One of the most important aspects of interpersonal communication, is active listening. A common misnomer of many people, is the assumption that if they are in the room, looking at the sender and responding, that alone automatically constitutes that they are actively listening. That is not necessarily, the case. **Active listening is demonstrated when a person prepares to listen** and gives observation to verbal and nonverbal messages that are being sent. Thought is then given to all of the input received, in order to respond appropriately to the message that has been presented.

When a leader engages in active listening, they are not only demonstrating attentiveness to the sender of the message, but equally as important, they are also demonstrating attentiveness to the message, to provide clear and appropriate feedback. Active listening ensures mutual understanding between the speaker or originator of the message and the listener or recipient.

The Monkey Island houses the radar, scanner and communication gear of a ship. It is located just above the Bridge and is at the topmost accessible height of the ship. The Bridge houses the navigation equipment and is the control center of the ship.

If the Monkey Island and the Bridge are out of sync, no voyage will be successful because both are necessary parts of the ship's operations and they must be able to effectively communicate with each other, in order to guarantee, that the ship will reach its intended destination.

Just as it is important for the equipment and parts of a ship to operate in tandem and to effectively communicate among and between themselves, so it is for the success of the leader's ship. To further demonstrate this principle, let's climb aboard Robert's organizational vessel.

Robert is the Senior VP of a Fortune 500 organization. He oversees all of the major operations and components of the business. There are 25,000 people in the organization. Robert is very aware of how his leadership affects the entire team and the outcomes of the company. As a result of this, he has developed a culture of interpersonal communication among the directors
and managerial teammates that he oversees. In his role, Robert has instituted a training module of active listening, as a part of the onboarding process for those who are hired or promoted into a director, managerial or supervisory role. At the initiation of his tenure, Robert also made it a part of required training for those who were already working for the company.

A part of this module focuses on differentiating which messages or information is best delivered face to face or by active telephone call, rather than via voicemail, email, or text messaging. He understands that some messages must be delivered to a massive group and therefore, email messaging is a

more efficient and effective way to deliver the message for clarity, later reference by the recipient and/or, as a time-saving measure. However, he is always considerate of what types of messages do not lend themselves to adequate feedback, such as an electronic or one-way communication mechanism, due to the lack of their ability to properly convey meaning, tone and sometimes, appropriate answers. When these critical pieces of communication are overlooked or deemed unimportant, misunderstandings and miscommunication are often the result.

Robert expects the attribute of active listening to be demonstrated by his managerial teammates, but he also makes a conscience effort to demonstrate the skill of active listening in his leadership and interactions. His philosophy is, "The worst type of communication, is miscommunication".

Effective communication builds trust, teammate enrichment, fulfillment and it facilitates and/or expands effective teams and team building.

Now that we have returned from our brief voyage aboard Robert's leader's ship, it may be beneficial for you to think about the following:

Leadership Probe:

1. How can I introduce or rekindle active listening in my organization?

Lead by example and you may want to consider a strategy to implement a required learning module, as Robert did.

2. How can I teach active listening as a trust building exercise during one of my next leadership retreats, seminars, events?

After you consider the culture of your organization, consider creating fun, but meaningful skits that demonstrate this or develop a game or activity wherein all participants have to rely on messages sent and received by a team member or group of team members and which requires them to work together to create a solution or to solve a problem to an everyday happening. Try to incorporate fun into this, without losing the essence of the idea relative to active listening that you are trying to convey. If you are not able to think of these activities, employ the help of another teammate (administrator, manager, other creative team member) to assist you with this.

3. Make a list of 2-3 things that you can do to begin or rekindle being an active listener as a leader. Be honest and patient with yourself. Give yourself time and room to grow. You can learn how to do this and to do it effectively. With practice, time and development.

So . . . are you ready to continue on this voyage to our next adventure?

Planning To Follow And Following The Plan – Strategizing

Now that you've effectively **"Brewed Your Crew"** and set up appropriate leadership channels for the organization that you're leading, you can focus on establishing, building upon or restructuring your plan of operations.

The Bridge, is the navigation and command station of a ship. The equipment contained in it, controls the speed and direction of the ship and monitors sea conditions and fixes the position of the ship, as previously mentioned. Managers, supervisors, directors of operations, HR, finance teams, etc., serve as the Bridge, of the leader's ship. They assist the leader with day to day operations, hiring team members/operating committees, implementation and creation of strategies, communicating, taking care of financial matters that impact the organization and with communicating pertinent information within the organization and with external partners and entities. They provide relevant information regarding business practices, direction, efficacy of execution, goal achievement, etc., without which, the leader cannot operate in their position, with optimal impact.

The insights and performance that these vital parts of "The Bridge" provide, must be sought after, utilized and should be well appreciated by the "Captain" (Leader). When this is demonstrated, fulfillment of purpose, goals, strategies and navigation, are readily recognized, resulting in a journey that is meaningful for everyone.

A useful strategic plan, consists of the following components:

    A. goals, modes and modalities, and mechanisms or methodologies of execution by which to accomplish the goals,

    B. a listing of necessary parts - people, departments, resources, tools, software products, partnerships, etc., that must be accessed or leveraged to meet the goals;

    C. risk management, which must be carefully observed while executing the strategic plan;

    D. timeframes, target dates for each goal and for the entire plan. This timeframe is usually 6-12 months. It may also be updated biennially.

Risks management is the tool or mechanism that an organization utilizes to mitigate its risks internally and externally.

It is recommended that every organization have a written risk management plan overall, outside of the strategic plan, for the general business in which it is involved. However, it should also be a part of the strategic plan to assess potential risks and damages that may be incurred, as a result of pursing the goals of the strategic plan, relative to a project or undertaking. The risk management portion of the plan is designed to mitigate potential operational, branding, risk of litigation, and financial risks. It should be a fluid document, just as the strategic plan is, which allows for careful management, observation and updates as necessary.

It is imperative that organizational leaders understand the correlation between the strategic and risk management plans and that everyone involved with the formulation and perpetuation of both plans, works together for the overall protection and preservation of the organization. If this is not understood and a key philosophy of operation, chaos may ensue. To better illustrate this, let's step into the conference room of a well-known business and listen in on the discussion that is currently, underway:

Elaine: "But Mark, I didn't think that your department needed to be aware of every step that we were taking in developing the new software. I thought that once you approved the budget, we were free to begin development and design and to work towards on time delivery of the product to the customer."

Mark: "My department did approve your original budget, however, material costs have escalated and delivery time for some of the resources you stated that you needed on your spreadsheet, are now one month later than expected. We have a promised delivery on this product instead of a proposed delivery date. Therefore, we lose 2% of our profit for every week that we delay on delivery." Mark replied. "Who did you have monitoring the risks on your team."

Elaine: "Robin. But I was certain that things were going ok and that we would have come in under or at budget, so I didn't double check our costs in a few areas. I wish that you would have included me or a member of my department in a few of your team monitoring sessions. We could have served as a form of checks and balances to support your team and ensure that we were moving forward in the right direction."

Mark: If I hadn't received your request for additional funds, I wouldn't have known that this was occurring."

Elaine: "My apologies Mark. I guess I really didn't understand the full necessity of the need to coordinate between departments on this, as much as I should have. So what can we do at this point?"

Mark: "We will need to do one of two things: Ask the customer for an extension, which will affect our profit margin. Or search for materials that may be compatible with the portion of the
product that has already been developed. Parts that may perform a similar function, even though it isn't exact. Either way, my department will need to recalculate changes in costs and check with our attorneys regarding the legalities of making these changes, in comparison to the original contract. No matter which choice we make, we have to come up with a new proposal to offer to the client, regarding the changes and updated date of delivery. We definitely can't deliver the product in the form of what they contracted us to create, on time. Transparency and open communication with them is our best approach. Let's get together tomorrow to discuss the new plan."

Elaine: "Ok, thanks, I appreciate it."

Sometimes, conflict resolution and the art of communication, do not go this smoothly. There are times when there is an impasse and no one is willing to work towards a solution, or the initial confrontation leads to more serious confrontations that are not easily managed. As the leader, you may have to step in and utilize your leadership and emotional intelligence skills (the capacity to be aware of, control and express one's emotions in interpersonal interactions fairly, justly and empathetically) to bring resolution to the matter. All of the skills mentioned here, may come into play when strategic and risk management plans are being developed and executed among teams.

Consistent and clear communication, as well as transparency, is necessary for targets to be reached and goals attained. Effective communication to an organization, is like fuel to the ship. It is necessary to keep the momentum of operations, going. It is not enough to simply, compose the plan. The plan must be understood, followed and adjusted as needed, in order to achieve smooth sailing. The leader must make sure that those who are aboard their ship, are planning to follow their leadership, and following the strategic and risk management plans.

Section III:

Successfully Navigating The Leader's Ship

Charting The Course

Now that the strategic and risk management plans have been developed or updated, it's time to chart the course. This step involves decision-making, relative to current and future actions the organization needs to take, in order to stay afloat competitively, and financially, in service to the community or in execution of its overall business practices.

During a voyage, the captain must ascertain what direction or route is necessary to successfully guide the ship toward its. intended destination. He or she, must have a clear understanding of the route, distance to be traveled, and knowledge of how well the ships' systems are working, all while giving oversight to the crew members, who are working to ensure that the ship arrives intact, where and when it should.

As the leader, you are the captain of the leader's ship, whether large or small, over which you have been given jurisdiction. It is imperative to understand how to direct your crew (your team members) towards meeting the benchmarks and goals outlined in the strategic and risk management plans. Unless you are an entrepreneur or leading a start-up, you may not formulate these plans on your own.

However, you still need to be aware of the information contained in the plans and have knowledge of the skillset you will need, in order to provide oversight and governance of the adequate execution of the plans.

Choosing the place to begin working on the goals and objectives of the organization, may be directed by the board, founder or executive leadership team. In some instances, the leader, may be called upon to make that decision, with input from stakeholders, managers, leaders, and teammates.

A ship will sink, if there are areas of damage or places where leaks go unnoticed or unchecked. The same is true of an organization that doesn't perform self-evaluations, assessments, and analyses on a consistent basis. Areas of initial consideration for charting the course, can be ascertained from such processes. We can learn more about this from Jaime.

Jaime, is a new executive director within her organization. She is eager to begin her tenure of leadership, but she wants to be effective in her role, from the start. She knows that she needs to rely on the wisdom and knowledge of teammates within the organization, in order to gain insight of past and present practices. Therefore, she sends out a survey, to find out perceived areas of need for improvement.

The survey consists of questions regarding operations, personnel retention and turnover, morale, and teammate satisfaction, as well as areas in which teammates feel they need more training to effectively fulfill their duties. Then she meets with stakeholders and asks similar types of questions, in addition to questions regarding where they would like to see increase or growth, information relative to the number of families served by the organization within the last 5 years, whether they feel that their overall goals were met or exceeded and perceived causes of shortfalls. After collecting all of this, Jaime meets with her administrative assistant to formulate this information into a chart format. She presents her collective findings to her leadership team, while allowing them to interject and ask questions throughout the presentation. She knows that obtaining buy in from
those who will be responsible for directly overseeing the work, is key and necessary. The team then decides on a strategic plan of execution based on this collaborative discussion. A follow-up, monthly meeting cadence is established to maximize accountability and continue strategizing and adjusting, as needed. To serve as a checks and balance system, departments whose work have overlap and similar functionality, are paired together as co-team members to achieve continued alignment with the charted course.

These combined processes, provide Jaime with incomparable knowledge and insight on how to adjust, monitor and chart the extended course for this organization. She makes herself available to leaders and supervisors, to connect with her, regarding questions they have between meetings or to assist with troubleshooting.

Charting the course is vital, but understanding where and how to begin the process, is critical to decreasing risks of costly mistakes, team burnout, and wasted time. With this information, the leader is able to continue sailing towards the organization's destination.

Leadership Probe:

1. **How can I determine how often to measure the efficacy of the plan initiated?**

It depends on the state of the organization at the time of the initiation of your leadership. A start-up and a well-established organization may share some of the same areas of need, but the urgency of the need will depend on whether or not, they are already successful, have a high rate of turnover or disengagement, are fiscally sound, deliver products and/or services that are in high demand, etc. The greater the level of need in any of these areas, the greater the need for monitoring progress and making repairs and enhancement adjustment.

2. **What do I do if there are no plans in place and I am the initial board chair, CEO, pastor, etc.?**

Always engage the wisdom and advice of others who have functioned or who are functioning in similar or the same role, that you are. Ask them for tips and suggestions, as well as toshare experiences on how they formulated their plans. If you are an entrepreneur, make sure that your goals and vision align. This will help you understand where to begin. Remember that purpose, goals and vision, go hand in hand; and that all are contingent upon the other.

3. **What do I do if my team or stakeholders want me to begin working on a certain area, but I know that the real issue lies with another area that needs to be repaired first or that is in a worse state than the area they are asking me to direct my attention to?**

Consider making a list of correlations between what you perceive should be the initial focus of repair and the area that you are being asked to start with. Request a meeting and demonstrate these comparisons in a manner that will make the listeners feel that you are addressing their concerns, while demonstrating the overlap and potential improvement that may result from a revamped focus. Examples include:

- Demonstrating how increasing pay scales may lead to greater retention and recruitment of people with more specialized skillsets.
- Demonstrating how increasing the organization's ability to achieve and retain cutting edge status within the industry will be a benefit and positive influence in garnering community and public support.
- Increasing the organization's ability to address additional areas of citizens' needs within the community, which may lead to increased visibility by potential community partners.

A Change Of Direction

Sometimes, the captain or a crew member, looks over the Bridge and determines that the direction of the ship, has to change. When waves are moving perpendicular to the ship, they can cause the direction of the ship to change, creating a new targeted direction, which differs from the destination that was planned when the ship left port. There are times when there must be an intentional shift or change of direction, due to the presence of icebergs, storms at sea or other vessels that are approaching. When a ship changes directions intentionally, it does so by a process called tacking. Tacking allows the bow to be turned through the wind. This action can assist ships in avoiding unintended peril and loss of the ship and to correct its current position, to be back on course.

When directional changes are made, delays, changes of schedule and time adjustments, may be experienced, if the changes are major. However, preservation of the lives onboard and the ship are the first and foremost concerns. New destinations also require directional shifts and changes. The same is true in an organization.

A change of focus, business concentration, community service offerings, realignment of goals and mission, rebranding, needed downsizing or expansion, are some of the reasons that a change of direction may come into play.

Change is not always easy and sometimes, it isn't very well accepted by those whose assignments, roles and responsibilities or involvement with the current flow of operation, are swept into the waves of uncertainty. In these instances, it is imperative to utilize transformational leadership skills. Just as the ship's captain must use everything at his or her disposal to turn the ship with the least amount of perceived discomfort to those on board. The leader must do the same when change of the leader's ship is inevitable and vital to the stability of the organization. The transformational leader will adjust his or her leadership style in order to implement the necessary changes, while as much as possible, giving careful consideration to the input and feedback of those who will be affected by the changes. Sometimes, these changes must be implemented, regardless of the anticipated fallout. In those cases, the leader can listen empathetically, but at the end of the day, they will have to choose what is best over what is easiest. Whenever possible, a wise leader takes the time to seek the expertise of team members who have extensive knowledge of the organization and the people involved, before implementing massive changes. However, they are also strong enough to execute changes, even when members of their executive leadership team are impacted or disagree.

A leader who is trying to be proactive, is also interested in the feasibility of the proposed changes, along with their financial implications and stress on those who must walk or work through them. Some viable questions to ascertain answers to, prior to putting the changes in place may include, but are not limited to the following:

1. Are the new mechanisms of operation doable and feasible, or do they just sound like a good idea?
2. Are they costs effective?
3. Will those who are executing the new plans, be overworked, resulting in frustration, teammate burnout, high turnover rates, or people being present, but not engaged?

These and additional questions that are derived, should be answered honestly, with a true assessment of possibilities, both positive and negative. Formulating a plan to address issues of concern regarding the proposed change of direction, can assist with troubleshooting, prior to change initiation. To better illustrate this, let's step into the boardroom of a local, well established foundation. Victor is the President and CEO and Bernice, is the board chair. Here is the scene that is unfolding as we enter the room:

Victor: "Bernice, we are in our 10th year of operation of the foundation and I know that we've accomplished a lot in the community and we've made some great strides. However, I am sensing that we may need to make some changes.

Bernice: "Ok, what kind of changes do you have in mind?"

Victor: "Well, I have been researching what some other foundations are doing around the country. Their focus is similar to ours in many ways and we have about the same number of members, but they are doing some things that we ae not and they are more successful at fundraising than we are. When I initially came up with the idea of starting a foundation, serving the community and making a difference, I was thinking of things in the direction we are currently operating. Now that we've grown into a foundation that has employees and some notoriety, I think that some changes relative to growth, focus on who we serve and how often, are needed. Of course, this will mean asking more of our employees, and possibly cutting some expenses and positions, to fund a project. These may be necessary steps that we will need to consider."

Bernice thought for a moment and gave him this response: "I understand that sometimes, a change of direction is necessary and can even be healthy or beneficial for an organization. However, I think that careful consideration of the answers to questions like:

1. What is the rationale for the change?

2. How far away from the purpose for which the community has known us to represent d depend on us for, are you willing to veer?

3. Are these changes necessary?

4. What is the operational risk of losing employees who are experienced, loyal and

whose skills are not easily replaced?

If we restructure, can the existing staff effectively manage the workload, without becoming burned out and if not, how many new hires will be needed? Do we have the

5. resources available to hire the necessary amount of new staff to support the new direction?

6. Will the culture and work environment of the foundation undergo positive or negative changes?

7. What is the targeted timeframe that you have in mind to present these proposed changes to the board?

These are just some of the questions that you will need to consider being prepared to answer. And believe me they will be asked! As well as some others, I'm sure, we haven't discussed or thought of yet."

Victor: "Thank you for your perspective, Bernice. I will think these things over, further assess and research them and be prepared to answer them before I discuss these possibilities with you, the next time we meet and in preparation for the board meeting."

Capsizing occurs when a ship leans too far to one side and it cannot regain its' previous position. This may occur if a ship losses stability due to speed, sudden turns, a cargo overload, or shift. Just as this may happen to an actual ship, the leader's ship may suffer the same fate, when decisions are made too hastily, without adequate research, thought or consideration of the potential impact to teammates. If there is no buy in from executive leadership or board members, or if the cost is not adequately or accurately calculated, PRIOR to implementation; if the organization takes on things that it is not equipped to handle.

If purpose of, or delivery from the organization changes, in a hasty, haphazard or negative way, in the eyes of stakeholders, community members, etc., organizational rupture or disaster may be the result.

To avoid this, careful thought, attention to details, and planning, as well as the true motives and reasons for the said changes, must be evaluated. It is not enough or advantageous to change directions of operations or focus, simply because another organization is doing the same. Timing of change is also a key factor in the relatability and efficacy of implementing change, which should also be well thought out, for optimal success.

Leadership Probe:

1. **If I am sure that a change of direction is needed, but I am receiving extensive push back, what should I do?**

Examine your reasons and motives for making changes. Make sure that they are valid and reasonable and that you can intelligently and adequately articulate your "whys", to others.

Ask the advice of a mentor who has dealt with having to make changes that were not well received. Ask questions regarding tips on presentation, best practices, timing, as well as how to

deal with questions regarding operational and relational fallout, etc. and ways that you can best deal with these occurrences.

2. What do I do if a predecessor changed the direction of the organization, which is now in recovery mode? How can I effectively handle the problems that I have inherited?

Try to gain a good understanding of where the organization use to be, why the changes were allowed and talk to stakeholders and owners regarding where they would like to see the organization move to. Use this information to formulate a 3-6 month strategic improvement plan with no more than 1-2 DOABLE goals. Include timelines and procedures to monitor gains in the areas targeted. Continue doing this until the organization is no longer operating in recovery mode and has moved to the level of a positive trajectory, stability and forward movement.

Understand that this damage will take time to repair. Rome was not built in a day. Accept that some things are not fixable. This is where you will need to use your leadership skills to discern and differentiate, this information. Try to salvage anything positive that you can and use it as a springboard for preparation to rebuild and rebrand, if and where necessary. Remember to take things, one step at a time.

Now that we have established that a change of direction may be necessary and we've examined the pros and cons and implemented or are working towards implementing the changes effectively, we're ready for smooth sailing . . . right?

Smooth Sailing . . . To Be Or Not To Be

"What happened", thought Melissa. "I have a great team, that understands its' assignments; and they were doing great work for the organization and in the community. The programs were funded and everything was on track, according to our strategic plan, but now, we're at a crossroads. Major decisions and revisions, will have to be made . . . all because of one, worldwide occurrence . . . COVID-19!"

Melissa's thoughts were, and still are being, echoed in numerous places around the world. From remote workers to Big Tech downsizing, to market shifts and more diverse needs within every community, leaders have had to and will for the foreseeable future, have to shift, strategize, critique, regroup, revamp, rebrand and in some cases, reinvent the ship that they are leading and themselves.

A captain must know how to navigate choppy waters and unfavorable weather conditions, which are not conducive to an enjoyable voyage. They may even have to have those aboard, disembark at another location, than what was previously planned.

The leader must be or become skilled at steering the leader's ship, in the waters of uncertainty and in some cases, into the unchartered waters of new developments, methodologies and everything from slight improvements, to radical change.

It is in these times, that the leader must rely on the input and expertise of teammates, extended outlooks and projections. It is imperative that the leader become more focused on stabilization and remaining afloat, with the least amount of collateral damage possible, then remaining fixated on what was or could have been. It is in these times that the leader must utilize and demonstrate a high level of emotional intelligence, so that decisions are made from a standpoint that will best anchor the organization and provide long standing stability, to avoid operational capsizing or running aground.

Following the information and tips outlined in this book or additional reading or training, will not provide a guarantee or transition of smooth sailing. As an actual ship must be steered, turned and undergo gravitational changes according to the conditions of the weather, atmosphere and even the ship itself, so the leader and their leader's ship, must have the adaptability to successfully navigate through the ever changing landscape of the business that it is in.

The skilled captain is a master of making the necessary adjustments to ensure the safety of the ship and all who are aboard it, to solidify and achieve their arrival at the intended destination.

The information in this book is designed to assist you in obtaining the skills needed or to enhance your existing skills, to assist you and your leader's ship, with reaching the destination of achievement, success and fulfillment.

Stay the course and you will arrive at unexpected and rewarding places in leadership and in life. HAPPY SAILING!!!

References

https://www.greatlakesmaritimejobs.org

https://www.noaa.gov

San Diego County Office Of Education

www.ingramcontent.com/pod-product-compliance
Lightning Source LLC
Chambersburg PA
CBHW050246220526
45465CB00002B/577